Charles Henry Wharton

**A poetical epistle to George Washington, esq.,**

Commander-in-chief of the armies of the United States of America

Charles Henry Wharton

**A poetical epistle to George Washington, esq.,**
*Commander-in-chief of the armies of the United States of America*

ISBN/EAN: 9783337731113

Printed in Europe, USA, Canada, Australia, Japan

Cover: Foto ©ninafisch / pixelio.de

More available books at **www.hansebooks.com**

# A POETICAL EPISTLE

TO

# GEORGE WASHINGTON, Esq.,

*COMMANDER-IN-CHIEF OF THE ARMIES OF THE UNITED STATES OF AMERICA.*

BY

REV. CHARLES HENRY WHARTON, D. D.

---

FROM THE ORIGINAL MANUSCRIPT BELONGING TO

DAVID PULSIFER, A. M.,

MEMBER OF THE NEW ENGLAND HISTORIC-GENEALOGICAL SOCIETY, FELLOW OF THE AMERICAN STATISTICAL ASSOCIATION, CORRESPONDING MEMBER OF THE ESSEX INSTITUTE, AND OF THE RHODE ISLAND, NEW YORK, CONNECTICUT, AND WISCONSIN HISTORICAL SOCIETIES.

WITH AN APPENDIX.

BOSTON:
PRINTED FOR DAVID PULSIFER.
FOR SALE BY A. WILLIAMS & CO.,
283 WASHINGTON STREET.
1881.

COPYRIGHT,
1881,
BY DAVID PULSIFER.

STEREOTYPED AT THE BOSTON STEREOTYPE FOUNDRY,
NO. 4 PEARL STREET.

PRINTED BY RAND, AVERY & CO., PRINTERS TO THE COMMONWEALTH,
NO. 117 FRANKLIN STREET.

TO THE MEMORY OF

# JOHN ALBION ANDREW,

Statesman, Magistrate, Orator, and

Lover of Men:

Governor of Massachusetts when the Nation's life was at stake, — who upheld the Union with all the power of the State and made the State felt at every fireside in the Union, — who by his clear insight was able to foresee, and by his wise forethought to prepare for, and with well-controlled enthusiasm and unchecked courage to meet, but never, by ill-judged haste, to precipitate the decisive issues of the war, — whose voice and pen were as eloquent as his intellect and manhood were dominant,

ONE WHOSE HAPPINESS IT IS

to have been so near him during that dreadful hour as to know how worthily, both as magistrate and man, within these walls, the silent witnesses of his labors, he stands in enduring marble by the side of

## WASHINGTON

HAS PRESUMED TO DEDICATE THIS LITTLE VOLUME.

State House,
*Boston*, February 22, 1881.

# CONTENTS.

|  | PAGE |
|---|---|
| POETICAL EPISTLE, | 7 |

### APPENDIX.

#### I.
An Account of the Author, . . . . . . 17

#### II.
Address of the Provincial Congress of Massachusetts to General Washington, July 1, 1775, . . . . . 24

#### III.
General Washington's Answer, . . . . . . 27

#### IV.
Celebration of August 14th, 1765, . . . . . 29

#### V.
Letter from General Washington to the Council, . . 31

#### VI.
Resolve of Congress, March 25, 1776: That the Thanks, in their own name and in the name of the Thirteen United

Colonies whom they represent, be Presented to His Excellency General Washington, and that a Medal of Gold be struck and Presented to His Excellency, . . . 33

### VII.

Address of the "Great and General Court or Assembly of the Colony of Massachusetts Bay," March 27, 1776, . 34

### VIII.

Answer, . . . . . . . . . . . 37

### IX.

Copy of Record of a Public Town Meeting in Boston, March 29, 1776, . . . . . . . . . 40

### X.

Address of the Supreme Executive Council of Pennsylvania, and Reply, . . . . . . . . 41

### XI.

Address of the Governor and Council of Massachusetts to the President of the United States, Oct. 27, 1789, . . 46

### XII.

Answer of the President, . . . . . . . 48

### XIII.

Address of the Hebrew Congregation in Newport, R. I., to the President of the United States, August 17, 1790, . 50

## CONTENTS.

### XIV.
The Answer, . . . . . . . . . . 53

### XV.
Statue of Washington in the State House, . . . . 55

### XVI.
Mr. Bryant's Last Poem, written Feb. 22, 1878, . . . 69

### XVII.
Report of the Celebration of Washington's Birthday in Switzerland, Feb. 22, 1879, . . . . . . 71

### XVIII.
Extract from the Speech of His Honor Moses Gill, Lieutenant-Governor of Massachusetts, Acting Governor, to the two Branches of the Legislature, January 10th, 1800, with Extracts from their Answers thereto, . . . . 81

### XIX.
Fac-simile of Memorial Tablets of the Washington family, in England, presented to the Commonwealth by Hon. Charles Sumner, . . . . . . . . 86

### XX.
Verses by Bishop Berkeley, on the Prospect of Planting Arts and Learning in America. . . . . . 105

# ABBREVIATIONS.

| | |
|---|---|
| B—tes | Butes. |
| Brit—c Maj—ty | Britannic Majesty. |
| Dunm—re | Dunmore. |
| G—l | General. |
| K—gs | Kings. |
| Mans—ds | Mansfields. |
| N—hs | Norths. |
| Roy—l | Royal. |
| W—n, Wash—n, Was—n | Washington. |
| Tyr—nic | Tyrannic. |
| Murd—d | Murdered. |
| Sand—h | Sandwich. |
| St. Ja—s | St. James. |

# A POETICAL EPISTLE

TO

*George W........n, Esqr., Commander in cheif of The Armys of the united States of America, from a Native of the Province of Maryland.*

> Ille Deūm vitam accipiet, Divisque videbit
> Permistos Heroas, et Ipse videbitur illis.   VIRG.

1778

The Reader may depend upon the following lines being the genuine production of a Native of America: The Author is not vain enough to flatter himself, that they will throw any fresh lustre on the character of General W——n; or entitle his untutored muse to the smallest share of Poetical fame. His sole view in penning this Epistle is to express in the best manner he is able, the warm feelings of a grateful Individual towards that best of men, to whom He & every American will in all likelyhood be principally indebted for the establishment of the Independence & commercial prosperity of their dear Country.

Philadelphia   ~~August 20~~ 1778

## A POETICAL EPISTLE TO GEORGE W——N, Esqr.
&c. &c.

While many a servile Muse her succour lends
To flatter Tyrants, or a Tyrant's friends;
While thousands slaughter'd at Ambition's shrine
Are made a plea to court the tuneful nine;
Whilst Whitehead * lifts his Hero to the skies,
Foretells his conquests twice a year, and lies,
Damns half starv'd Rebels to eternal shame,
Or paints them trembling at Britannia's name;
Permit an humble Bard, Great Cheif, to raise
One truth-erected trophy to thy praise.
No abject flat'ry shall these numbers seek
To raise a blush on Virtue's modest cheek,
Rehearse no merit, no illustrious deed,
But Foes must own, & W——n may read.

First, where along yon venerable wood,
My native stream † swells thy Potomack's flood,

* Poet Laureat to his Brit—c Maj—ty, & obliged from his office to discover in his Roy-l Patron matter of praise twice in the year.
† The River Wicomaco in the Province of Maryland.

These artless lines shall usher in the song,
Which millions yet unborn in rapture shall prolong.

Fair Freedom too, great Source of ev'ry bliss,
That man can taste in other Worlds or this,
Retiring exiled from yon Eastern climes
May deign, perhaps, to listen to these rimes;
And on these plains well pleas'd to find relief,
May bear them smiling to her fav'rite Chief.

Yes, happy Man! Thee with one common voice
Thy Country chose, & Freedom bless'd the choice.
Forth from the bosom of thy calm retreat,
At once the Hero's & the Sage's seat,
Where lavish Nature spreads her choicest gifts
Of woods & lawns along thy Native cliffs;*
Where with the Graces Wisdom chose to roam,
Where sweet Simplicity had fixt her home,
Where wedded Love display'd his mildest ray
To guild each rising & each setting day,
And with a smile could smooth the brow of care
Save when thy Country's cries alarm'd thy ear,
The Goddess call'd Thee to the glorious strife,
She bad Thee quit the peaceful walks of life;

\* The Cliffs of Virginia.

And made Thee Guardian of the mighty Cause,
Whilst ev'ry sister Province shouts applause.

Thus, when of old, from his paternal farm
She bad the rigid Cincinnatus arm;
Th' illustrious Peasant rushes to the feild,
Soon are the haughty Volsci taught to yeild;
His Country sav'd, the solemn triumph o'er,
He grubs his native acres as before.

Or when Timoleon's godlike bosom glow'd
To court true fame, & Virtue mark'd the road;
Joyful she led him to Trinacria's\* shore
And Kings & Kinglings quickly were no more.
On his firm aid fair Syracusa calls,
And from his throne, lo! Dyonisius falls.
Yet Tyrant-like, ambitious still to rule,
He struts the petty Monarch of a school:
Whilest Thee, illustrious Cheif, no titles grace,
Save Friend & Guardian of the human race.
Hail happy man! crown'd with immortal bays,
Before whose glory shrink the dazzling rays
Of Royal pageantry; thy gen'rous heart
To Freedom's sons shall still its warmth impart,

\* Sicily.

Teach them their native dignity to scan,
And scorn the Wretch who spurns his fellow man.
And when in eastern Climes 'midst lawless sway,
Thy fame shall sink & Freedom's wreaths decay,
These infant States shall catch the godlike flame,
And tyrants still shall shudder at thy name:
O Yes Columbia,* dare but to be free,
And what Timoleon was, thy W———n shall be.

What, tho proud Britain yet undrench'd with blood
Pour her destructive thousands o'er the flood,
What, tho' the spoils of some defenseless coast
Swell dull Gazettes or feed the *Morning Post;*
What, tho with fierce pedantic proclamation
Some future Burgoine scare this *puny* nation;
Rouze the grim Savage to relentless war,
And scarce persuade his scalping arm to spare;
What, tho' fresh wreaths more bloody vict'rys twine
To grace thy temples, Gates, or Arnold, thine;
What, tho' Herculean labours still remain,
And ev'ry battle must be fought again;
Yet, if th' embattled field thy Genius guide,
Or at the Senate Wisdom still preside,
Sooner shall yon blew mist-clad Mountain † dread

---

* America.
† A very lofty mountain on the confines of Maryland call'd Blew Ridge.

The rattling storms that war around his head,
Sooner shall night usurp the beam of day
Than freedom crouch to slav'ry's iron sway:
Calm and serene Columbia views the storm
Whilest her brave youth around thy standard swarm,
Each bosom panting for the glorious wreath,
Or, should they fall, each grasping it in death.

   Come, then Ye minions of tyr—nic sway
Strive who shall best its dire Commands obey:
Once more fierce Vaughan lead forth thy savage band,
And scatter desolation thro' the land,
Once more let Hudson mourn his rifled plains
His ravish'd daughters, and his murd—d swains;
Or, if in British cheifs there still should dwell
Souls black as that, which Dunm—re cull'd from hell;
Ev'n thy Virginia, Wash——n, may view
Her Infants bleed, her Norfolks blaze anew:
All this may be; the blood already spilt
Fills not, perhaps, Britannia's cup of guilt:
Stern disappointment still her arm may brace
To aim at vengeance by some fresh disgrace;
Or, may not Heav'n still eager to disclose
Th' unconquer'd mind, that in Thy bosom glows,
Dangers on dangers heap, new labours raise
'Till in full lustre all thy virtues blaze:

'Till led by Thee, the brave untutor'd band
Chase hardy Vetrans from this injur'd land;
'Till mighty Clinton at thy trophies bow,
Or sink unnotic'd as a Gage, or Howe;
'Till hapless Britain curse the fatal hour,
When urged by Pride & insolence of pow'r,
She, sternly deaf to ev'ry meek petition
Thought with a frown, to look us to submission.
Alass! poor Britain! thus thy Sand——h spoke,
And eager Senates caught the dreadful joke:
Yankees & Dastards now congenial names,
Amuse the Lord of catch-clubs, or St. Ja—s
Each pension'd scribbler draws his servile pen
And proves Americans are hardly men;
Each strives revenge, or laughter to create
From Don Pomposo,* down to Parson Bate,†
And with this *gospel* pray'r each pulpit rings,
Heav'n! spare not Rebels to the *best* of K—gs.

Such was thy folly, Britain, such thy fate,
Thus sink the Selfish, Insolent & Great,
Of heav'nly vengeance doom'd to feel the rod,
Who dare deride great Nature & her God.

\* The Great Dr. Johnson Author of *Taxation no Tyranny*.
† The Rev'd Editor of an edifying paper called the *Morning Post*.

Far other thoughts, Columbia, be thy Pride,
Far other springs thy public councils guide :
Thine be the godlike Task, the Glory Thine
First to adopt & spread the flames divine
Of wide Benevolence ; her gentle star
Shall light the rescued millions from afar ;
Sweetly invite them on these plains to find
The great Azylum of oppress'd mankind,
Then to their eyes unfold the wondrous plan
Where the poor slave shall read that He is *Man*,
Taste Freedom's charms more pure than Rome could boast,
Or Albion, once her fav'rite Isle has lost.

Great without pomp, without Ambition brave,
Proud not to conquer fellow-men, but save ;
Friend to the wretched, Foe to none, but those
Who plan their greatness on their Brethren's woes ;
Aw'd by no titles, faithless to no trust,
Free without faction, obstinately just ;
Too rough for flatt'ry, dreading ev'n as death,
The baneful influence of Corruption's breath ;
Warm'd by Religion's sacred genuine ray
That points to future bliss th' unerring way,
Spurning as Hell, grim Superstition's laws
Too long a Tyrant in the noblest cause ;

The World's great mart, yet not by gold defil'd,
To mercy prone, in Justice ever mild,
Save to the man, who saps great Freedom's roots;
And never cursed with Mans—ds, N—hs, or B—tes.
Such be my Country; what her Sons should be,
O, may they learn, great Was——n, from Thee!
Thy patriot virtues be th' enlighten'd rule,
Thy public conduct be the Patriot school
Brighter than precept; whence her rising youth
May gather Wisdom, Constancy & Truth,
Of independence catch the gen'rous flame,
And shudder early at Oppression's name.

And when retiring late from earthly cares
Thy better part shall mount her native spheres
Midst Patriot Cheifs to quaff the pure delight
Of ever thinking, speaking, acting right;
O still thy fame shall guide this fav'rite race!
Some bold Macauley's faithful pages grace,
Or flow expanded down the stream of time
The darling subject of immortal rime:
Such as rehears'd Pelydes' fatal ire,
Such as great Milton echo'd to thy lyre,
Or that sweet Bard's, who sung the man that bore
His course to Latium from the Trojan shore.*

* This line is from Pitt's translation of Virgil.

Then Commerce here shall fix her cheif abode
And thy Potomack heave beneath the load
Of crowding fleets, each crew in grateful lays
Thro' their rough throats shall pour thy deathless praise,
And pointing to Mount Vernon * shall relate,
There once lived Wash—n, the Good, the Great
Pride, Love, & Saviour of this mighty State:
Yon noble structures rose at his command,†
Yon waving Groves were planted by his hand;
There pensive would he roam, or in yon bow'r
Reclin'd, would plan his Country's bliss & pow'r:
In Camps, in Senates this his constant aim,
That her great cause, & Nature's be the same:
That here with Virtue, Science, Justice reign,
And Freedom rear her everlasting Fane.

July 10, 1778.

---

\* The General's seat on the Potomac River, a few miles below Alexandria.

† 'Tis said the G——l intends building an elegant house at Mount Vernon.

# APPENDIX.

## I.

### AN ACCOUNT OF THE AUTHOR.

THE author, in a short sketch of his life, written by himself, and published after his decease in the first volume of "The Remains of the Rev. Charles Henry Wharton, D. D., with a memoir of his life, by George Washington Doane, D. D., Bishop of the Diocese of New Jersey," published at Philadelphia, M DCCC XXXIV, says:

"I was born in St. Mary's county, in the province, now the state, of Maryland, on the 25th day of May, O. S. [answering to our 5th of June] in the year 1748. The family plantation is called Notley Hall. It had been the residence of a Governor of that name; and was presented to my grandfather by Lord Baltimore, towards the close of the 17th century. From him, it descended to my father, Jesse Wharton; and, at his death in 1754, it became my property, and continued so until I took orders in the Roman Catholic Church, and then I conveyed it to my brother, — after whose death it became the property of his son, C. H. Wharton, now residing in Washington. My mother was Anne Bradford, descended, like my father, from one of the respectable and first settlers in the province. She was a woman of sweet manners and of uncommon beauty: and many of her maternal precepts and tender caresses are still fresh in my memory and frequently present her dear image to mind."

"In the year 1760, I was sent to the Jesuits' College at St. Omers, a seminary at that time very deservedly celebrated for teaching the Greek and Latin classics with great accuracy, and for its strict discipline in all literary and religious duties. My master, or preceptor, was the Rev. Edward Walsh, to whom, as a most amiable and affectionate man, as well as a good classical scholar, I was attached by the most unlimited confidence, and the warmest sentiments of gratitude and love.

"In 1763, the English College was broken up at St. Omers, and the officers, teachers and scholars retired to the city of Bruges in Flanders, where they received the protection and encouragement of the

Austrian government. It was there that I completed my classical education, under the instruction and tuition of my beloved master, Mr. Walsh. Sequestered from' all society beyond the walls of the College, and of course a total stranger to every thing unconnected with the strictest discipline in acquiring classical attainments, and those habits of devotion, which were deemed essential to a Roman Catholic youth, I applied myself very diligently to my studies, and became prominent among my associates, in a very accurate knowledge of the Latin language, which became nearly as familiar as English, as we were obliged to converse in it during our ordinary relaxations from our studies."

At the latter end of the war of the American Revolution, he was residing in Worcester, in England, in the capacity of Chaplain to the Roman Catholics of that city. When this residence commenced cannot be determined. He was deeply interested on the side of his country, and anxious to return. In the year 1778, as appears at the end of the manuscript, he wrote the Poetical Epistle to General Washington, which was printed for the benefit of the American Prisoners. The first of a series of letters addressed to him at that place and continued until the time of his departure for America, is dated March, 1777. The letters were written by a fellow countryman, in the confidence and employment of the British government; and evince in both of them an ardent love of civil liberty, and a deep and glowing sympathy with their brethren in America, who were engaged in that desperate struggle by which its triumphs were achieved. A prominent subject of this correspondence was the publication, for the benefit of the American prisoners, of the "Poetical Epistle." His correspondent, in a letter dated Nov. 2, 1778, after stating that the poem had been criticised by Sir William Jones, (calling him "the celebrated Persian Jones,") and that he had procured a print from Paris of General Washington, but as it was "a front face and only of bust size," he had got the distinguished painter, Benjamin West, "to promise to make a fulllength drawing, in order to get a print engraved," adding, "but the artists in that way ask such a confounded deal of money, that I doubt if my finances will allow me to get it struck off." In a later letter (14th April, 1779,) he writes: "I am inclined to think if this is done,"— the poem published, with a life and character of General Washington,— "and a proper dedication to some distinguished personage, (suppose the Duchess of Devonshire, for she particularly distinguished him as a toast at her table,) it may sell for half a crown or two shillings. Mr. West has formerly seen General Washington, and I think, with my recollection of him and description of his face, a drawing may be made tolerably like him, so that a small full length may be got for the frontispiece of a quarto edition. I have spoken to West about it, but he cannot think of anything else but two pictures he is finishing, for the exhibition, which opens the 24th instant." . . . . " think also of a dedication. The Duchess has befriended the American prisoners, and the mention that the poem is published solely to raise a little money for our imprisoned brethren, whose distresses have been very great, may lead to a good sale of the book."

In the year 1782 the author left the Church of Rome. He returned to this country in 1783. In 1798, he was ordained Rector of St. Mary's Church, Episcopal, at Burlington, N. J., where he died, July 23d, 1833, in the 86th year of his age.

In the memoir of his life, by George Washington Doane, D. D., his biographer says: "I have not been able to find a copy of this publication, though much inquiry for it has been made. From one of the manuscript copies found among the papers of the author, the English publication seems to have been a re-print from an edition printed in Philadelphia, in 1778, by J. Bradford. But this opinion I have not been able to substantiate. Whatever may be thought of its poetical merits, the benevolent purpose for which it was published must commend it to the general favour."

In an appendix to the memoir, his biographer adds: " In Dr. Wharton there was a rare combination of great and varied excellencies. In purity of mind and heart he was almost like an infant. His character was transparent in its beautiful simplicity. He was a personification of that loveliest attribute of love, 'charity *thinketh no evil.*' Among the very first (by confession of all) of American divines, revered and honoured by all who ever knew him, he was the humblest and most diffident of men. He seemed not only unconscious of his distinction, but incapable of its consciousness. There was in him, as nearly as in humanity there can be, an absorption of the principle of self. He had literally learned, in whatsoever state he was, to be therewith content. To all mankind his heart overflowed with kindness and charity. He was emphatically a man of peace. His charities were constant, generous, and unostentatious. He was the most tender and affectionate of husbands. Constitutionally reserved, and rendered more so by education and early habits, he associated intimately with but few. To them he was the most agreeable of companions and the most engaging of friends. He was the lover of little children, and of course beloved by them. In sickness and in sorrow he was prompt and assiduous as the minister of consolation. The poor rise up and call him blessed. The tears of a whole congregation were mingled in his grave." —DAVID PULSIFER.

## II.

## ADDRESS

OF THE PROVINCIAL CONGRESS OF MASSACHUSETTS.
July 1, 1775.

*To his Excellency George Washington, Esqr., General and Commander in Chief of the Continental Army.*

*May it please your Excellency:*

The Congress of the Massachusetts Colony, impress'd with every Sentiment of Gratitude and Respect, beg leave to congratulate you on your safe arrival: and to wish you all imaginable Happiness and Success, in the execution of the important duties of your elevated station. While we applaud that Attention to the public good, manifested in your Appointment, we equally admire that disinterested Virtue, and distinguished Patriotism, which alone could call you from those Enjoyments of domestic Life, which a sublime & manly Taste Joined with a most affluent Fortune can afford, to hazard your Life, and to endure the fatigues of War in the Defence of the Rights of Mankind, and the good of your Country.

The laudable zeal for the common Cause of America, and Compassion for the Distresses of this Colony, exhibited by the great dispatch made in your Journey hither, fully justify the universal Satisfaction we have, with pleasure, observed on this Occasion; and are promising Presages that the great Expectations formed from your personal Character, and military Abilities are well founded.

We wish you may have found such Regularity and Discipline already established in the Army, as may be agreeable to your Expectation. The Hurry with which it was necessarily collected, and the many disadvantages, arising from a suspension of Government, under which we have raised, and endeavoured to regulate the Forces of this Colony, have rendered it a work of Time. And tho' in great measure effected, the Completion of so difficult, and at the same time so necessary a Task is reserved to Your Excellency; and we doubt not will be properly consider'd and attended to.

We would not presume to prescribe to Your Excellency, but supposing you would choose to be informed of the general Character of the Soldiers who compose this Army, beg leave to represent, that the greatest Part of them have not before seen Service. And altho' naturally brave, and of good understanding, yet for want of Experience in military Life, have but little Knowledge of divers things most essential to the Preservation of Health and even of Life. The Youth in the Army are not posses'd of the absolute Necessity of Cleanliness in their Dress, and Lodging, continual Exercise, and strict Temperance, to preserve them from Diseases frequently prevailing in Camps; especially among those, who, from their Childhood, have been us'd to a laborious Life.

We beg Leave to assure you, that this Congress will at *all times*, be ready to attend to such Requisitions as you may have Occasion to make to us; and to contribute all the Aid in our Power, to the Cause of America, and your Happiness and Ease, in the Discharge of the Duties of your exalted Office.

We most fervently implore Almighty God, that the Blessings of Divine Providence may rest on you. That your Head may be cover'd in the Day of Battle: That every necessary Assistance may be afforded; and that you may be long continued in Life, and Health, a Blessing to Mankind.

## III.

### GENERAL WASHINGTON'S ANSWER TO THE ADDRESS.

*Gentlemen,*

Your kind Congratulations on my Appointment, & Arrival demand my warmest Acknowledgements, and will ever be retained in grateful Remembrance.

In exchanging the Enjoyments of domestic Life for the Duties of my present honourable, but arduous Station, I only emulate the Virtue & public Spirit of the whole Province of Massachusetts Bay, which with a Firmness, & Patriotism without Example in modern History, has sacrificed all the Comforts of social & political Life, in Support of the Rights of Mankind & the Welfare of our common Country. My highest Ambition is to be the happy Instrument of vindicating those Rights, & to see this devoted Province again restored to Peace, Liberty & Safety.

The short Space of Time which has elapsed since my Arrival does not permit me to decide upon the State of the Army — The Course of human Affairs forbids an Expectation, that Troops formed under such Circumstances, should at once possess the Order, Regularity & Discipline of Veterans — Whatever Deficiences there may be, will I doubt not, soon be made up by the Activity & Zeal of the Officers, and the Docility & Obedience of the Men. These Qualities united with their native Bravery & Spirit will afford a happy Presage of Success, & put a final Period to those Distresses which now overwhelm this once happy Country.

I most sincerely thank you, Gentlemen, for your Declarations of Readiness at all Times to assist me in the Discharge of the Duties of my Station: They are so complicated, & extended that I shall Need the Assistance of every good Man, & Lover of his Country; I therefore repose the utmost Confidence in your Aid. In Return for your affectionate Wishes to my-self permit me to say, that I earnestly implore that Divine Being in whose Hands are all human Events, to make you & your Constituents, as distinguished in private, & publick Happiness, as you have been by ministerial Oppression, by private & publick Distress.

Go. Washington.

## IV.

[Celebration of August 14th, 1765.]

CAMBRIDGE AUGUST 14TH, 1775.

THIS day the Field Officers of the 6th Brigade under the command of Colo. James Frye met at the House of Jonathan Hastings Esqr. to celebrate the memorable 14th of August when the following toasts were drank vizt.

1st  The Continental Congress.
2d  Success to our undertakings.
3d  The memorable 14th Augt. 1765.
4th  May American valor ever prove invincible to the attempts of Ministerial tyranny to oppress them.
5th  The 12 United States.
6th  All our Friends in Great Britain.
7th  Liberty without Licentiousness.
8th  A speedy & happy conclusion to the present unhappy dispute.
9th  The 29th of April.
10th  A speedy entrance possession & opening of the Town of Boston.

11th The President of the Continental Congress.

12th General Washington & the other Genl Officers of the American Army.

13th A speedy export to all the enemies of America without any Draw Back.

14th Immortal Honor to that Patriot & Hero Doctor Warren, & the Brave American Troops who fought the Battle on the 17th of June, 1775.

## V.

### LETTER FROM GENERAL WASHINGTON TO THE COUNCIL.

CAMBRIDGE 6TH DEC'R 1775.

Copies of the Inclosed Letter I have already written to the Governors of Rhode Island & Connecticut, & shall do the same to the President of the Congress in New Hampshire; as I conceive our Affairs are in a very critical Situation. —

It was mentioned to me yesterday, in conversation, that the Militia of this Government ordered in, to supply the place of the Connecticut Troops, are allowed 40s pr month, of 28 days. — The first I highly approv'd of, because I was unwilling to see any inviduous distinction in pay; the never failing consequence of which is, jealousy, & discord — But Sir, if the Genl Court of this Colony have resolved on the latter, you must give me leave to add, that it aims the most fatal stab to the Peace of this Army that ever was given; & that, Lord North himself, could not have devised a more effectual blow to the Recruiting Service.

Excuse me Sir for the strength of these expressions — if my Information is wrong (I had it from Gen'l Heath, who says he had it from a Member of your Court) they are altogether Improper & I crave pardon for them. If right, my Zeal in the American cause must plead my Excuse. — I am with great respect Sir

   Y'r Most Obed't H'ble Ser.
      Go. WASHINGTON.


Superscribed
  On the Service of the
   United Colonies.

To
  The Hon'ble the President
 of the Council
     Massachusets Bay.

## VI.

### IN CONGRESS.

MONDAY, MARCH 25, 1776.

*Resolved*, That the thanks of this Congress, in their own name, and in the name of the thirteen United Colonies, whom they represent, be presented to his excellency general Washington, and the officers and soldiers under his command, for their wise and spirited conduct in the siege and acquisition of Boston; and that a medal of gold be struck in commemoration of this great event, and presented to his excellency; and that a committee of three be appointed to prepare a letter of thanks, and a proper device for the medal.

The members chosen, Mr. J. Adams, Mr. Jay, and Mr. Hopkins.

## VII.

### ADDRESS

OF THE "GREAT AND GENERAL COURT OR ASSEMBLY OF THE COLONY OF MASSACHUSETTS BAY," MARCH 27, 1776.

*To his Excellency George Washington Esq'r General and Commander in Chief of the Forces of the United American Colonies.*

*May it please your Excellency:*

When the Liberties of America were Attacked by the Violent hand of Oppression: when Troops, Hostile to the Rights of humanity Invaded this Colony, seized our Capital, and spread havoc and destruction around it; when our virtuous Sons were Murdered, and our Houses destroyed by the Troops of Britain: The Inhabitants of this and the other American Colonies impelled by self preservation and the love of Freedom, forgetting their domestick concerns, determined, resolutely & Unitedly to oppose the Sons of Tyranny.

Convinced of the Vast importance of having a

Gentleman of great Military Accomplishments to discipline, lead and conduct the Forces of the Colonies, it gave us the greatest Satisfaction to hear that the Hon'ble Congress of the United Colonies, had made choice of a Gentleman thus qualified, who leaving the Pleasures of domestic and Rural life was Ready to undertake the Arduous task — And your Nobly declining to accept the pecuniary Emoluments annexed to this high Office, fully evinced to us that a Warm Regard to the Sacred rights of humanity and sincere love to your Country, solely Influenced you in the acceptance of this Important Trust.

From your Acknowledged Abilities as a Soldier and your Virtues in public & private life, we had the most pleasing hopes, but the fortitude & Equanimity so conspicuous in your conduct: the wisdom of your Councils, the Mild, yet strict Government of the Army, your attention to the civil Constitution of this Colony, the regard you have at all times shown for the lives and health of those under your Command, the fatigues you have with Chearfulness endured, the Regard you have shewn for the preservation of our Metropolis, and the great address with which our Military Operations have been conducted, have exceeded our most sanguine expectations and demand the warmest returns of Gratitude. —

The supreme Ruler of the Universe having smiled on our Arms and crowned your labours with Remarkable Success, we are now, without that Effusion of Blood, we so much wished to avoid, again in the quiet possession of our Capital: the Wisdom & prudence of those movements which have Obliged the Enemy to abandon our Metropolis, will ever be Remembered by the Inhabitants of this Colony.

May you still go on approved by Heaven, revered by all good Men, and dreaded by those Tyrants who claim their Fellow men as their property — may the United Colonies be defended from Slavery by your Victorious Arms — may they still see their Enemies flying before you — and (the deliverance of your Country being effected) may you in retirement, enjoy that peace & satisfaction of mind which always attends the good & great. And may future Generations, in the peaceful Enjoyment of that Freedom, the Exercise of which your sword shall have established raise, the Richest and most lasting Monuments to the Name of Washington.

## VIII.

### GENERAL WASHINGTON'S ANSWER.

[Entered on the Records by order of the General Court, April 1, 1776.]

*Gentlemen:*

I return you my most sincere & hearty thanks for your polite address: and feel myself called upon by every principle of Gratitude, to acknowledge the Honor you have done me in this Testimonial of your approbation of my appointment to the exalted station I now fill; and what is more pleasing, of my conduct in discharging its important duties.

When the Councils of the British Nation had formed a plan for enslaving America, and depriving her Sons of their most sacred & invaluable privileges, against the clearest Remonstrances of the Constitution — of Justice — and of truth: and to execute their schemes had appealed to the sword — I esteemed it my duty to take a part in the contest, and more especially, when called thereto by the unsolicited suffrages of the Representatives of a free people; wishing for no other reward than that arising from a conscientious discharge of the important trust, and that my Services might contribute to the Establishment of Freedom and peace, upon a permanent foundation ; and merit the applause of my Countrymen and every virtuous Citizen.

Your professions of my attention to the civil constitution of this Colony, whilst acting in the line of my department, also demand my grateful thanks — A Regard to every Provincial institution, where not incompatible with the common Interest, I hold a principle of duty & of Policy, and shall ever form a part of my conduct — had I not learned this before, the happy experience of the advantages resulting from a friendly intercourse with your Honorable body — their Ready and willing Concurrence to aid and to counsel whenever called upon in cases of difficulty and Emergency would have taught me the useful lesson.

That the Metropolis of your Colony, is now relieved from the cruel and oppressive invasion of those who were sent to erect the standard of lawless domination, and to trample on the Rights of Humanity, and is again open & Free for its rightful possessors, must give pleasure to every virtuous and Sympathetic heart — and being effected without the Blood of our Soldiers, and fellow Citizens must be ascribed to the interposition of that providence, which has manifestly appeared in our behalf thro' the whole of this important struggle, as well as to the measures pursued for bringing about the happy event.

May that being who is powerful to save, and in whose hands is the fate of Nations, look down with an Eye of tender pity and compassion upon the whole of the United Colonies — May he continue to smile upon their councils and Arms, and crown them with success, whilst employed in the cause of Virtue & of Mankind — May this distressed Colony & its Capital, and every part of this wide, extended Continent, through his divine favour, be Restored to more than their former Lustre and once happy State, and have peace, liberty & safety secured upon a Solid, Permanent ; & lasting foundation.

GEORGE WASHINGTON.

## IX.

At a Meeting of the Freeholders and other Inhabitants of the Town of Boston, duely qualified & legally warned in public Town Meeting assembled at the old Brick Meeting House, on Friday the 29th Day of March Anno Dom. 1776

The Town brought in their Votes for a Moderator of this Meeting, & upon sorting them it appear'd that

The Hon'ble Thomas Cushing Esq. was chosen unanimously, who took the chair, & made a Congratulatory Speech to the Inhabitants, upon the Recovery of the Town out of the hands of the British Enemy, & for the present Opportunity of transacting the Affairs & business of the Town in a free Town Meeting.

## X.

# ADDRESS

OF THE SUPREME EXECUTIVE COUNCIL OF PENN-
SYLVANIA.

*Sir:* — The President and Supreme Executive Council of Pennsylvania cheerfully embrace this interesting occasion to congratulate you upon the establishment of the Federal Constitution, and to felicitate ourselves and our country upon your unanimous appointment to the Presidency of the United States.

In reflecting upon the vicissitudes of the late war, in tracing its difficulties and in contemplating its success, we are uniformly impressed with the extent and magnitude of the services which you have rendered to your country, and by that impression we are taught to expect that the exercise of the same virtues and abilities which have been thus happily employed in obtaining the prize of Liberty and Independence, must be effectually instrumental in securing to your fellow citizens and their posterity the permanent blessings of a free and efficient government. And although the history of the Revolution will furnish the best evidence of the invariable attachment of this Commonwealth to the interests and honor of the Union, yet we cannot resist this favorable opportunity of personally assuring you that in every measure which tends to advance the national character, you may rely on the zealous co-operation of the executive authority of Pennsylvania.

In discharging the duties of your present important station it must, sir, be a never failing source of consolation and support, that the unbounded love and confidence of the people will produce a favorable construction of all your actions, and will contribute to the harmony and success of your administration. For we know that eventually your happiness must depend upon the happiness of your country, and we believe that in wishing an adequate execution of your intentions and designs we comprehend all that is necessary to both.

Uniting with our sister States in the admiration of those motives which at this interesting æra of our affairs have induced you again to relinquish the enjoyment of domestic peace, for a conspicuous and laborious participation in the cares and toils of public life, we fervently pray for the preservation of your health, and we confidently hope that the consummation of a patriot's wishes — the glory and felicity of your country will crown the period of a long and illustrious existence, and prepare you for an everlasting reward. THOMAS MIFFLIN, *President*.

COUNCIL CHAMBER, PHILADELPHIA, April 18th, 1789.

---

The Council met.

PHILADELPHIA, Tuesday, April 21st, 1789.

The President reported that the address which was agreed to on the eighteenth instant, was this morning presented to the President of the United States, and that he was pleased to make the following reply, vizt:

TO THE PRESIDENT AND SUPREME EXECUTIVE COUNCIL OF PENNSYLVANIA.

*Gentlemen :*— I receive with great satisfaction the affectionate congratulation of the President and Supreme Executive Council of Pennsylvania, on my appointment to the Presidency of the United States.

If under favor of the Divine Providence, and with

the assistance of my fellow citizens, it was my fortune to have been in any degree instrumental in vindicating the liberty and confirming the independence of my country, I now find a full compensation for my services, in a belief that these blessings will be permanently secured by the establishment of a free and efficient government, and you will permit me to say on this occasion, that as nothing could add to the evidence I have formerly received of the invariable attachment of your Commonwealth to the interests and honor of the Union ; so nothing could have been more agreeable to me at this time, than the assurances you have given me of the zealous co-operation of its Executive authority, in facilitating the accomplishment of the great objects which are committed to my charge.

While I feel my sensibility strongly excited by the expressions of affection and promises of support, which I every where meet with from my countrymen, I entertain a consolatory hope that the purity of my intentions and the perseverance of my endeavors to promote the happiness of my country, will atone for any of the slighter defects which may be discovered in my administration. For whatever may be the issue of our public measures, or however I may err in opinion, I trust it will be believed that I could not have been actuated by any interests separate from those of my country.

Suffer me, gentlemen, to conclude by assuring you that I am well pleased with the Justice you have done to the motives from which I have acted, and by thanking you for the tender concern you have been pleased to manifest for my personal felicity.

GEORGE WASHINGTON.

## XI.

## ADDRESS

OF THE GOVERNOR AND COUNCIL OF THE COMMONWEALTH OF MASSACHUSETTS, TO THE PRESIDENT OF THE UNITED STATES.

*Sir*,

We meet you at this time, with our hearts replete with the warmest affection and esteem, to express the high satisfaction we feel in your visit to the Commonwealth of Massachusetts.

We can never forget the time, when, in the earliest stage of the war, and the day of our greatest calamity, we saw you at the head of the army of the United States, commanding troops determined, though then undisciplined, by your wisdom and valor preventing a sanguinary and well appointed army of our enemies from spreading devastation through our country, and sooner than we had reason to expect, obliging them to abandon the capital.

We have since seen you in your high command, superior to the greatest fatigues and hardships, successfully conducting our armies through a long war, until our enemies were compelled to submit to terms of peace, and acknowledge that independence which the United States in Congress assembled had before asserted and proclaimed.

We now have the pleasure of seeing you in a still more exalted station, to which you have been elected by the unanimous suffrages of a free, virtuous and and grateful country. From that attachment which you manifestly discovered while in your military command, to the civil liberties of your country, we do assure ourselves that you will ever retain this great object in view, and that your administration will be happy and prosperous.

It is our earnest prayer that the divine benediction may attend you here and hereafter ; and we do sincerely wish that you may, through this life, continue to enjoy that greatest of earthly blessings, to be accepted by the multitude of your brethren.

COUNCIL CHAMBER, BOSTON, October 27, 1789.

## XII.

## THE ANSWER.

To his Excellency the Governor and the Honourable the Members of Council of the Commonwealth of Massachusetts.

*Gentlemen:*

TO communicate the peculiar pleasure which I derive from your affectionate welcome of me to the Commonwealth of Massachusetts, requires a force of expression beyond that which I possess. I am truly grateful for your goodness towards me, and I desire to thank you with the unfeigned sincerity of a feeling heart.

Your obliging remembrance of my military services is among the highest compensation they can receive; and, if rectitude of intention, may authorize the hope, the favourable anticipations which you are pleased to express of my civil administration, will not, I trust be disappointed.

It is your happiness, Gentlemen, to preside in the councils of a Commonwealth, where the pride of independence is well assimilated with the duties of society, and where the industry of the citizens gives the fullest assurance of public respect and private prosperity. I have observed too, with singular satisfaction, so becoming an attention to the Militia of the State, as presents the fairest prospects of support to the invaluable objects of national safety and peace. Long may these blessings be continued to the commonwealth of Massachusetts! And may you, Gentlemen, in your individual capacities, experience every satisfaction which can result from public honour and private happiness.

G. WASHINGTON.

BOSTON, October 27, 1789.

## XIII.

## ADDRESS

Of the Hebrew Congregation in Newport, Rhode Island, to the President of the United States of America.

*Sir,*

Permit the children of the stock of Abraham to approach you with the most cordial affection and esteem for your person and merit, and to join with our fellow-citizens in welcoming you to Newport.

With pleasure we reflect on those days — those days of difficulty and danger, when the God of Israel, who delivered David from the peril of the sword, shielded your head in the day of battle; and we rejoice to think, that the same Spirit who rested in the bosom of the greatly beloved Daniel, enabling him to preside over the provinces of the Babylonish empire, rests, and ever will rest, upon you, enabling you to discharge the arduous duties of Chief Magistrate in these States.

Deprived as we heretofore have been of the invaluable rights of free citizens, we now (with a deep sense of gratitude to the Almighty Disposer of all events) behold a government erected by the Majesty of the People — a government, which to bigotry gives no sanction — to persecution no assistance ; but generously affording to all, liberty of conscience, and immunities of citizenship : deeming every one, of whatever nation, tongue or language, equal parts of the great governmental machine. This so ample and extensive Federal Union, whose base is philanthropy, mutual confidence, and public virtue, we cannot but acknowledge to be the work of the Great God, who ruleth in the armies of heaven, and among the in-inhabitants of the earth, doing whatsoever seemeth him good.

For all the blessings of civil and religious liberty, which we enjoy under an equal and benign administration, we desire to send up our thanks to the Ancient of Days, the Great Preserver of men, beseeching him that the Angel who conducted our forefathers through the wilderness into the promised land, may graciously conduct you through all the difficulties and dangers of this mortal life. And when like Joshua, full of days and full of honours, you are gathered to your fathers, may you be admitted into the heavenly paradise, to partake of the water of life, and the tree of immortality.

   Done and Signed by order of the Hebrew Congregation, in Newport, (Rhode Island).

      MOSES SEIXAS, Warden.

NEWPORT, August 17, 1790.

## XIV.

### THE ANSWER.

To the Hebrew Congregation in Newport Rhode Island.

*Gentlemen,*

While I receive with much satisfaction your Address, replete with expresssions of affection and esteem, I rejoice in the opportunity of assuring you, that I shall always retain a greatful remembrance of the cordial welcome I experienced in my visit to Newport, from all classes of citizens. The reflection on the days of difficulty and danger which are past, is rendered the more sweet from a consciousness that they are succeeded by days of uncommon prosperity and security.

If we have wisdom to make the best use of the advantages with which we are now favoured, we cannot fail, under the just administration of a good government, to become a great and happy people.

The citizens of the United States of America, have a right to applaud themselves for having given to mankind examples of an enlarged and liberal policy: a policy worthy of imitation. All possess a like liberty of conscience, and immunities of citizenship. It is now no more that toleration is spoken of, as if it was by the indulgence of one class of people that another enjoyed the exercise of their inherent natural rights. For happily the government of the United States, which gives to bigotry no sanction, to persecution no assistance, requires only that they who live under its protection should demean themselves as good citizens, in giving it on all occasions their effectual support.

It would be inconsistent with the frankness of my character, not to avow that I am pleased with your favourable opinion of my administration and fervent wishes for my felicity. May the children of the stock of Abraham, who dwell in this land, continue to merit and enjoy the good will of the other inhabitants — while every one shall sit in safety under his own vine and fig-tree, and there shall be none to make him afraid.

May the Father of all Mercies scatter light and not darkness in our paths, and make us all in our several vocations useful here, and in his own due time and way everlastingly happy.

G. WASHINGTON.

## XV.

STATUE OF WASHINGTON IN THE STATE HOUSE.

*To the Honourable the Senate and House of Representatives, &c., &c., &c.*

Respectfully represent the Undersigned, being a Committee of the Trustees of the Washington Monument Association, that at the last June Session of the Honorable Legislature permission was given to the Trustees, by a Resolve to place the Statue of Washington in the Doric Hall of the State House. At that time the Statue was not finished nor had the eminent Sculptor, F. Chantrey, Esquire, in whose hands it was, then expressed his Opinion or wishes, with regard to its ultimate location. Among the several places mentioned for its erection, the Doric Hall was considered by some as the most eligible; and the Trustees deemed it expedient to obtain leave to place it there, in case it should arrive before the following session of the Legislature, and the Association should then upon further examination be satisfied to give it that destination. Within a few weeks the Statue has arrived, and remains as yet unopened, and the Trustees are anxious to afford the Public the gratification of viewing it, as soon as a suitable place for its exhibition can be provided. On further consideration, however, the Trustees have become satisfied, that there are some serious objections to placing the Statue in the Doric Hall, arising chiefly from its great extent, cross lights and direct interference with its occasional uses. A room bearing a certain proportion to the figure, of an appropriate color, and admitting the light in one direction, is thought to be necessary to exhibit it to the greatest advantage. Mr. Chantrey himself, whose wishes it was thought proper to consult, and whose opinion is entitled to the highest respect, has requested that the Statue should not, under any circumstances, be placed before a Portico, or in an open Temple, because, as he remarks, there would be no light to show it to advantage. Every citizen of Massachusetts would be desirous that the Statue of Washington should lose nothing of its dignity, beauty, or effect, by being seen in a bad light or placed in disadvantageous position. Under these impressions, the Committee respectfully request permission of this Honorable Legislature to erect a Semicircular Room, on the North front of the

State House, to be connected, by the central door, with the Doric Hall. Such a structure, on the North side of the State House, of about sixteen feet in heighth, and projecting about twenty-four feet, would be, it is believed, rather an Ornament than a blemish, while it would afford every advantage for the most perfect exhibition of the Statue. To aid the judgment of the Legislature, however, upon this point, the Committee have prepared plans and drawings of the proposed room, which they are ready to submit to their inspection. The funds of the Association are believed to be fully adequate to the expence of erecting such a structure, including the Pedestal, with other incidental expences and under the impression, that the final disposition of the Statue, herein suggested, is the best, the Committee in behalf of the Trustees ask permission to carry their design into execution, with the advice and co-operation of the Legislature, to be given in such manner as they shall deem expedient.

WARREN DUTTON  
JAMES LLOYD  
JNO DAVIS  
EDWARD EVERETT  
JOHN LOWELL

## COMMONWEALTH OF MASSACHUSETTS.

IN SENATE, June 8th, 1827.

On the Petition of the Trustees of the Washington Monument Association,

*Resolved*, That permission be hereby given to the Trustees of the Washington Monument Association to erect, at their own expence, a suitable building on the north front of the State-House, for the reception & permanent location of the Statue of Washington, by Chantrey — and that said building shall be of such materials, and construction, as His Excellency the Governor shall sanction & approve — and when completed & the Statue placed therein, His Excellency, the Governor, is hereby authorised & requested to take all such measures as may be needful & proper for its preservation & safe keeping.

*In Senate*, June 8, 1827
 Read twice and passed
  Sent down for Concurrence,
   JOHN MILLS, President.
*House of Representatives*, June 12, 1827
 Read and passed in concurrence
   WM. C. JARVIS,
    Speaker.
*June* 12th 1827,
 Approved
   LEVI LINCOLN

## EXTRACT

### FROM THE GOVERNOR'S MESSAGE.

"The members of the Legislature have, at this time, the gratification of personally witnessing the execution of the Resolve of the 12th of June last, which authorized the erection of a suitable building for the reception and permanent location of the Statue of Washington, by the Artist CHANTREY, procured at the cost and under the direction of the Washington Monument Association. The Trustees of that Association have accomplished the interesting commission with which they were charged, in a manner alike honorable to themselves, and satisfactory to the public. A splendid specimen of the arts, and an enduring memorial of grateful remembrance to noble virtues and patriotic services, is seen in the Statue, which now adorns this Edifice. Henceforth, the image of *him* "*who was first in the hearts of his Countrymen,*" will be sensibly present in the halls of the government, with the representatives and servants of the people, to keep constantly alive in their minds the recollection of his precepts and farewell injunctions, and to animate them in the performance of public duty, by the teachings of his example forever. No other place was so suited to the position of this grand and impressive object. It will here remind us all, of our obligation to country. It will reprove in us, and those who shall come after us, so long as a virtuous sentiment shall remain to respect the consecrated marble, every disloyal and unpatriotic feeling. It will instruct *Rulers* how they are responsible to the people, and the *People*, what should be the character of their Rulers. It will speak more eloquently than tongues of the pre-eminence of the civic virtues; of the sovereignty of the laws; of reverence for the Constitution; of the inviolability of the Union.

To the Washington Monument Association, not only is the *Country* indebted for the possession of the Statue, but *this Commonwealth*, most especially for its location and the entire expense of the appropriate and elegant Room which has received it. The pecuniary benefaction has amounted to the considerable sum of *sixteen thousand dollars*, and as the result of an elevated spirit of liberality, it should be borne in grateful and perpetual remembrance."

Levi Lincoln.

Council Chamber, Boston, January 2, 1828.

## MESSAGE.

*Gentlemen of the Senate and*
*Gentlemen of the House of Representatives*

I hasten to lay before You a Communication from the President and Trustees of the Washington Monument Association, conveying a formal expression of their bestowment of the Statue of Washington, upon the Government And People of this Commonwealth.

The Letter addressed to me, on the Subject, altho' of earlier date, was not received in season to admit of its transmission with the documents, which accompanied my Message this Morning.

LEVI LINCOLN

COUNCIL CHAMBER
Jan'y 2d, 1828

## LETTER FROM THE PRESIDENT AND TRUSTEES OF THE WASHINGTON MONUMENT ASSOCIATION.

BOSTON, December 20, 1827.

*To*
*His Excellency Levi Lincoln*
*Governor and Commander in Chief of the*
*Commonwealth of Massachusetts*

SIR,

The Trustees of the Washington Monument Association have the honour to inform your Excellency that the edifice erected by them by permission of the Government of Massachusetts and upon a plan approved and sanctioned by your Excellency has been completed in a style worthy of the character of the State, and that the noble Statue by Chantrey, an illustrious Artist, has been happily without accident or injury placed therein.

A more appropriate situation could not have been selected, than a beautiful Hall connected with the Seat of Legislation of a State, which had the glorious privilege of making the earliest resistance to oppression, and in relieving the Capital of which, Washington first displayed, in our revolutionary struggle, that consummate wisdom and prudence which contributed so essentially to our final success. Long may this Monument of public gratitude remain as a stimulus to our rulers in future times to emulate the rare virtues of the immortal Washington.

We have the honour of transmitting to your Excellency the Act of the Trustees formally ceding and confiding the care of the Hall of Washington and of the Statue to the Government of the State. The Provisoes annexed to the Act of Cession are such as must be approved by every admirer of the Father of his Country. The Hall was calculated in its dimensions for one figure only, and however great the merits of other patriots, there is such an unmeasurable distance between Washington and all others, that all must agree, that he should stand alone. The Provision that it should not be removed from Boston is not only equitable because seven eighth parts of the Subscription were furnished by Citizens of that town, but the original articles of Association having expressly provided for the erection of a Statue in the Capital of the State, it must be considered as part of the contract with the Subscribers, from which the Trustees are not legally authorized to depart.

To your Excellency we respectfully submit the mode of making this Communication known.

We have the honour to subscribe ourselves,
Respectfully
Your Excellency's h'ble Servts

ISRAEL THORNDIKE *President*
JOHN LOWELL, *Vice President*

WARREN DUTTON
  by J. Lowell

WM PRESCOTT
P. C. BROOKS *Treas'r*

JOHN C. WARREN    DANIEL SARGENT
JOSIAH QUINCY    JNO. DAVIS
T. H. PERKINS    I. P. DAVIS
NATH'EL BOWDITCH    BENJ'N RUSSELL

At a meeting of the Trustees of the Washington Monument Association, held in the hall consecrated to the memory of the Father of his Country, on Monday the 26th of November 1827.

Whereas: The Hall erected by permission of the Legislature of Massachusetts in the rear of the State House for the reception of the Statue of Washington has been completed at the expence of the Trustees aforesaid, and the Statue of Washington has been placed therein.

*Voted:* That the Trustees of said Association by virtue of the powers vested in them, do confide and entrust as well the said edifice erected at their expence, as the noble Statue, the work of the first Artist in Europe, to the care and patriotism of the Government of the State of Massachusetts for the use and benefit of the People of said State to all future generations, with the following provisoes, that the said Hall shall never be appropriated to any other use, or the exhibition of any other Monument or work of Art than the Statue of Washington, and that in case the edifice of which the Hall of Washington forms a part shall at any future time cease to be used for the purposes to which it is now devoted The Trustees of the Washington Monument Association or their Successors or in failure of them the Mayor and Aldermen of the City of Boston for the time being shall have a right to take possession of the Statue of Washington and its pedestal and to remove the same to any other situation within the City of Boston which they may deem appropriate.

Attest: ISRAEL THORNDIKE, *President*.

*Secretary.*

Ordered that the foregoing Communication be recorded, Copies having been transmitted to both Branches of the Legislature.

LEVI LINCOLN.

COUNCIL CHAMBER, Jan'y 2d 1827.

## COMMONWEALTH OF MASSACHUSETTS.

*In the year of our Lord one thousand eight hundred and twenty-eight.*

WHEREAS the Trustees of the Washington Monument Association have passed the following vote: "At a meeting of the Trustees of the Washington Monument Association, held at the Hall, consecrated to the memory of the Father of his country, on Monday the 26th of November 1827.

"WHEREAS the Hall erected by permission of the Legislature of Massachusetts in the rear of the State House for the reception of the Statue of Washington has been completed at the expense of the Trustees aforesaid; *Voted:* that the Trustees of said Association, by virtue of the power vested in them do confide & entrust, as well the said edifice erected at their expense, as the noble statue, the work of the first artist in Europe, to the care & patriotism of the Government of the State of Massachusetts, for the use & benefit of the people of said state to all future generations, with the following provisoes:— That the said Hall shall never be appropriated to any other use or the exhibition of any other monument or work of art than the Statue of Washington, & that in case the edifice of which the Hall of Washington forms a part, shall at any future time, cease to be used for the purposes, to which it is now devoted, the Trustees of the Washington Monument Association or their successors, or in failure of them, the Mayor & Aldermen of the City of Boston, for the time being, shall have a right to take possession of the Statue of Washington, and its pedestal & to remove the same to any other situation within the city of Boston, which they may deem expedient."

Therefore *Resolved:* That the Legislature of this Commonwealth accepts the Statue of Washington upon the terms and conditions, on which it is offered by the Trustees of the Washington Monument Association; and entertains a just sense of the patriotic feeling of those individuals, who have done honour to the State by placing in it a statue of the man, whose life was among the greatest of his country's blessings, and whose fame is her proudest inheritance.

*In Senate* Jan'y 4, 1828
    Read & passed, sent down for concurrence.
                    JOHN MILLS, *President*

*In House of Representatives*, January 8, 1828.
Read and Concurred.

WILLIAM C. JARVIS, *Speaker*

January 9th 1828.

Approved,

LEVI LINCOLN.

## XVI.

The following tribute to the memory of Washington, is taken from the SALEM REGISTER of June 24th, 1878:

MR. BRYANT'S LAST POEM.

Mr. Bryant's literary life extended over a period of seventy-four years. In 1804, at the age of ten, he printed his first poem in a Massachusetts country paper, and on February 22, 1878, he wrote his last poem as a contribution to the Washington's Birthday number of the Sunday School Times of Philadelphia. The memory of Washington has never received so worthy a tribute from an American poet as the six noble stanzas given below:

THE TWENTY-SECOND OF FEBRUARY.

BY WILLIAM CULLEN BRYANT.

Pale is the February sky,
   And brief the mid-day's sunny hours;
The wind-swept forest seems to sigh
   For the sweet time of leaves and flowers.

Yet has no month a prouder day,
    Not even when the summer broods
O'er meadows in their fresh array,
    Or autumn tints the glowing woods.

For this chill season now again
    Brings, in its annual round, the morn
When, greatest of the sons of men,
    Our glorious Washington was born.

Lo, where, beneath an icy shield,
    Calmly the mighty Hudson flows!
By snow-clad fell and frozen field
    Broadening the lordly river goes.

The wildest storm that sweeps through space
    And rends the oak with sudden force,
Can raise no ripple on his face,
    Or slacken his majestic course.

Thus, 'mid the wreck of thrones, shall live
    Unmarred, undimmed, our hero's fame;
And years succeeding years shall give
    Increase of honors to his name.

## XVII.

WASHINGTON'S BIRTHDAY IN SWITZERLAND.

THE one hundred and forty-seventh anniversary of the "Father of his Country" was celebrated at the Hotel National at Geneva on the 22d of February, 1879, when were present distinguished representatives of every European nation, with the single exception of Turkey, the American Consul, Major Montgomery, presiding. From a Report of this celebration, published in the Geneva Times, of February 26th, 1879, a copy having been kindly brought to me by Hon. Robert S. Rantoul, the following extracts are taken.

---

After a considerable time spent in agreeable gustatory and colloquial exercises, the American Consul called for order and proposed to close the sitting at the table in the good old-fashioned American manner, with a little after-dinner talk. He then spoke eloquently as follows:

### REMARKS OF THE PRESIDENT.

We are assembled here to-night, as you are aware, to commemorate the one hundred and forty-seventh

Anniversary of him who was first in war, first in peace and first in the hearts of his countrymen. And here I desire to remark that it is to me, as it must be to all Americans here present, a source of no little pride and gratification to find ourselves surrounded by the Representatives of so many of the Powers of Europe, and citizens of different Nationalities, all of whom have willingly and gladly come to unite with us in doing honor to him who so justly wore the soubriquet of "the Father of his country." I accept this as first evidence of the cordial relations which exist between our respective Governments, and I am sure that I echo the sentiments of all my fellow-countrymen, when I add that this international friendship is cordially appreciated, and we say in all sincerity, *esto perpetua!*

Ladies and gentlemen, it is not my purpose nor is it neccessary to eulogize the character of our illustrious first President. The simple story of his life, his untiring devotion to duty, his heroic sacrifices and his peaceful retirement to the more congenial pleasures of domestic scenes, is the noblest eulogy which could be written, and no language, if mine had the power of the most gifted of orators, could intensify the imperishable halo which encircles his honored name and perpetuates his undying glory.

From the days of the great Alexander down through the long lapse of centuries to our own modern times, the pages of history are filled with the names of warriors, heroes, and statesmen whose deeds have shed lustre upon the ages in which they lived or who have astonished the world by their skill, powers, and diplomacy, but the pages of the same history can be searched in vain for a character which combined so much of the heroic, and resolute; the gentle and the mild. It resembled a shaft of pure Pentelic marble built upon a foundation of firm, enduring granite. Washington lived solely for his country and his country's good, and, flinging away ambition, died as he had lived, a Christian hero and patriot, bequeathing to posterity a name which all Americans revere, and which people of all civilized nations place in the highest niche of human greatness and excellence.

I feel that I cannot draw a better peroration to these few remarks than by quoting a verse from a beautiful ode by one of England's favorite poets:

" Land of the West! though passing brief the record of thine age,
Thou hast a name which darkens all on history's wide page.
Let all the blasts of Fame ring out, thine is the loudest far!
Let others boast their satellites, thou hast the planet star!

Thou hast a name whose characters of light shall ne'er depart !
'Tis stamped upon the dullest brain, and moves the coldest heart!
A war-cry fit for any land where Freedom's to be won !
Land of the West ! it stands alone ! it is thy Washington !"

The Consul was greeted with applause, and closed with the first toast of the evening, " The Memory of Washington," which was received in silence, the company rising.

The second toast, " The President of the United States," was responded to by Mr. Robert S. Rantoul of Massachusetts, who spoke as follows:

### Response of Mr. Rantoul.

Mr. Consul: You have proposed to this gathering of mingled nationalities the health of the President of the United States of America. And you have devolved it upon me to return the thanks of my countrymen for the manner in which that sentiment has been responded to.

The President of the United States, ladies and gentlemen, is a shifting personality. In the magistrate, the American sees an embodiment of the august idea of Liberty, as coupled with that of Order, and Progress, and Power, and Law. In the man, who fills that exalted station to-day, the American sees, — and it is fitting that I should say it in this presence, — the American sees an Executive who, in point of personal purity and honor, and in breadth of feeling for the country, has a right to sit in the chair of Washington. (Applause.)

Mr. Chairman: The President of the United States is the central figure of fifty millions of people, drawn together from every quarter of the habitable globe. You might bring here more flags than we see folded in fraternal harmony to-night, — you might bring them until we beheld

> "In concord furled,
> The war flags of a gathered world,"

but not one flag would you find among them all that had not danced before the boyish vision of some citizen of America as the ensign of his native land. Drawing our population, therefore, from all nations, we are the natural friends and kindred of all nations. To all alike we wish prosperity and peace and we ask only their good-will and blessings in return. We seem to see, in our country, an instrument of conciliation, amity, and peace. For it has been permitted us to behold the nationalities of the earth, coming together under the genial sunshine of our Republic, to fuse themselves into one harmonious people, — respecting one another's traditions, — guaranteeing one another's rights, — even as the flags of the nations that wave their war-worn folds with the Stars and Stripes to-night, find themselves in union with each other because we are in friendship with them all. (Bravos and applause.)

I thank you, ladies and gentlemen, for the unanimity with which you have received a sentiment so dear to Americans.

### Remarks of M. Vautier.

The third toast was to "Switzerland." Mr. Vautier, President of the Canton de Genève, stated that he was not entitled to speak for the Confederation, but would reply as a Swiss and as a citizen of Geneva. The memory of Washington had come down to us without a spot. While the First Consul had stifled the Republic, Washington considered himself honored to be the first President of his liberated country.

To the fourth toast, "The Queen of Great Britain," Mr. Auldjo, British Consul, responded as follows :

Mr. Consul, Ladies and Gentlemen : In rising to address you at the request of your chairman, I do not presume to return thanks for the toast of the health of Her Majesty the Queen, which you have just drank. With us, as I have on former occasions explained, it is neither the custom nor etiquette for any one to return thanks for the compliment paid to his Sovereign. But called upon by your chairman to speak I obey his command. I think it was very becoming and very considerate of you, Mr. Chairman, and your committee for this celebration, to invite the British residents to take part in it. It however has been asked, Why should you have done so? And also, Why are we here? I will tell you why this invitation had its peculiar fitness. You remembered, as we remember, that on the 22d February, 1732, there was born in Virginia a British subject who was destined to shed an undying lustre both on the old and the new country, and that British subject was George Washington. During the earlier part of his life, he was a brave, loyal, hard-working servant of the Crown, and as a Colonial soldier fought the battles of his country against its invading foes, the French and Indians. And he so distinguished himself, that eventually holding the King's commission commanding the Royal and Colonial troops, he led them to signal victory on the Banks of the Ohio, and freed the State from the invading foe. Bravest of the brave he was ever in the thickest of the fight, yet so extraordinary was his escape from wound, that history tells us the pastor of his parish, from the pulpit, expressed a belief that Providence had spared him in this manner for some more important service to his country, and as we all know, it was so. It was not his fault that he was driven to war against his King. Can you suppose it was by the mere doctrine of chance that the bigoted obstinacy of the Sovereign, and the ill-advised counsels of his ministers should have attempted to impose on an intelligent people unnecessary taxes — the obnoxious stamp-act and oppressive duties, until they drove it to desperation and resistance.

No! was it not rather in the progress of evolution and the fitness of things that this attempted pressure should in the hands of Providence be the means of creating a nation, one of the greatest, and in all probability about to be the greatest on the face of the globe. But to lead this resistance a man was wanted — strength of character, great prudence and rectitude of conduct pointed out George Washington to be that man.

I am not going to give you the history of that resistance — of the War of Independence, its reverses and its crowning success at Saratoga and Yorktown. Most of you know it, and those who do *not*, may learn it all in the columns of to-day's *Swiss Times*. Suffice it for me to say that George Washington was the living corner-stone of the Great Temple of Freedom, which was erected on the other side of the Atlantic, and over which floated the national banner of the stripes and stars — the banner we see before us to-night.

When Washington saw that the temple was firmly erected, he felt his work was done, and returned to his home and into the ranks of the private citizen. Not long to remain there indeed, for when the storms and dissensions surrounded the newly-launched bark of the Republic, he was summoned forth again to take the helm and be the Pilot to guide it to port. That done, he again sought his "ain fireside," which he loved so well.

Washington was indeed a great commander, but as has been said of him he never aspired to be an Alexander or a Cæsar. What he aspired to be was that noblest work of God, an honest man.

You cannot, then, be surprised that we, as well as yourselves, sisters and brothers of America, are proud of this man, well knowing that the blood which flowed in his veins was British blood, that it was the British feeling of indomitable repugnance to all tyranny that animated his whole conduct. It is this knowledge that brings us here cordially to join you in the celebration of this day, believing your George Washington — our George Washington — to have been the most single-hearted, most unambitious, most virtuous patriot that ever adorned the annals of history.

## XVIII.

### EXTRACT

From the Speech of His Honor Moses Gill, Lieutenant Governor of Massachusetts, Acting Governor, to the two Branches of the Legislature, January 10th, 1800, with Extracts from their Answers thereto.

"*Gentlemen of the Senate and
Gentlemen of the House of Representatives*

VERY soon after you began your last Session we were called to the melancholly task of performing the funeral obsequies of the Chief Magistrate of this Commonwealth.* The unfeigned sorrow, universally exhibited on that occasion, evinced the strong affection of his fellow citizens. His memory still lives, and the lenient hand of time has not yet erased it from my breast.

We are now called upon to lament the loss of another Patriot, General GEORGE WASHINGTON,

* Increase Sumner, who died June 7, 1799.

whose invaluable life was the ornament, example and defence of our Nation; and whose name itself was a Host. — But WASHINGTON is dead! — and we sorrow most of all that we shall see his face no more; for GOD hath changed his countenance and sent him away. May the recollection of his virtues stimulate; — and the force of his sentiments inspire the whole Nation with a love of patriotism and national glory. The tears of the great and the good of all countries are mingled with those of *America* on this unsearchable dispensation of Divine Providence. May our tears on this occasion embalm his precious memory. MOSES GILL.

JANUARY, 10th, 1800.

---

EXTRACT FROM THE ANSWER OF THE SENATE.

SCARCELY had we reconciled ourselves to part with the weeds, which, as an emblem of the grief of our hearts, we had assumed, from respect to the memory of our late excellent Governor, when our sorrows were again called forth by the death of General GEORGE WASHINGTON. Most sincerely do we deplore with you this common calamity of our country, and of the human race. His very name afforded security to our peace and prosperity, and his eminent qualities made him an example to the great ones of the earth. — While it becomes our nation humbly to submit to this afflictive dispensation of Providence, no means can so effectually repair their misfortune, as a general imitation of his virtues, and a practical observance of the invaluable counsels which he has left them.

## EXTRACT FROM THE ANSWER OF THE HOUSE OF REPRESENTATIVES.

"SCARCE had the tear, which had bedewed the the cheek of Patriotism upon the death of our much honoured Chief Magistrate, been dried away: His passing knell was but just expiring in our ears, when our feelings were again agonized with the afflictive intelligence of the loss of our Country's Father, Protector and its first best human friend. The eloquence of unaffected grief is silence: and were we to indulge the feelings of our hearts, we should mourn in forcible but dumb expression. — But to the prejudices and usages of mankind we owe some respect, and, therefore, in language as brief as it is incompetent, we will speak his Eulogy. To call WASHINGTON a Hero, would be a debasement of him; for Heroism has been hitherto too often allied with crime. To call him merely a great Soldier, would be injustice; for *he* fought not to destroy but to preserve. To denominate him simply a great Statesman would be inadequate; for his politics were not like those of most Statesmen, subservient to his ambition. In War, he united the coolness of FABIUS with the spirit of CÆSAR and the humility of CINCINNATUS. In Peace, he blended the virtues of TRAJAN with the wisdom of SOLON and the sublime prophetic ken of CHATHAM. Uniform and consistent in his Political conduct, with equal severity he frowned on the intrigues of Domestic Faction and the insidious wiles of Foreign Artifice. Equally ready to draw his sword in his ripened manhood, to establish the Independence of his Country, and in his declining years to snatch it from its sleeping scabbard to avenge its insulted Honor and violated Rights. The watchful Father and the illustrious Founder of a great Empire, he did not strive to invest himself with the insignia of Nobility, the ordinary ambition of vulgar greatness; but by his talents and virtues he has

ennobled his Country. The mortal part of WASH-
INGTON is consigned to the silent cemetery, but he
hath bequeathed to his beloved Fellow Citizens a
glorious Legacy, in his Example, his Character and
his Virtues, which ought to render them pure and
virtuous in their Morals, devout in their Religion,
fervent in their Patriotism, just in the Cabinet,
and invincible in the Field. Four millions of Free-
men, with melancholly hearts, are living statues to
thy memory, thou sainted Patriot! Unfading lau-
rels, fair as thy Virtues and imperishable as thy fame,
shall bloom around thy Monument, and protect, from
unhallowed touch, thy consecrated Urn!

## XIX.

## FAC-SIMILES

OF THE

MEMORIAL STONES OF THE LAST ENGLISH ANCESTORS

OF

## GEORGE WASHINGTON

IN THE PARISH CHURCH OF BRINGTON, NORTH-
AMPTONSHIRE, ENGLAND;

PERMANENTLY PLACED IN THE

STATE HOUSE OF MASSACHUSETTS.

---

COMMONWEALTH OF MASSACHUSETTS.

EXECUTIVE DEPARTMENT, COUNCIL CHAMBER, }
BOSTON, March 15, 1861. }

*To the Honorable the House of Representatives:*

I have the honor to present to the General Court, as a gift to the Commonwealth of Massachusetts from one of its citizens, certain memorials of great historic interest.

The home and final resting-place of the ancestors of GEORGE WASHINGTON were until recently unvisited by, and unknown to, Americans. In the genealogical table, appended to the "Life of Washington" by our distinguished fellow-citizen, Mr. Jared Sparks, it is stated that Lawrence Washington, the father of John Washington, (who emigrated to Virginia in 1657,) was buried at Brington; but though both Mr. Sparks and Washington Irving visited Sulgrave, an earlier home of the Washingtons, neither of these learned biographers appears by his works to have repaired to this quiet parish in Northamptonshire.

Our fellow-citizen, the Hon. Charles Sumner, on a recent visit to England, identified certain inscriptions in the parish-church of Brington, near Althorp, as being those of the father and uncle of John Washington, the emigrant to Virginia, who was the great-grandfather of the Father of his Country.

Earl Spencer, the proprietor of Althorp, so honorably known as an early advocate of Parliamentary reform, sought out the quarry from which, more than two centuries ago, these tablets were taken, and caused others to be made which are exact *fac-similes* of the originals. These he has presented to Mr. Sumner, who has expressed the desire that memorials so interesting to all Americans, may be placed where they may be seen by the public, and has authorized me to offer them to the Commonwealth if it be the pleasure of the legislature to order them to be preserved in some public part of the State House.

I send with this a letter addressed to myself by the learned historian of Washington, bearing testimony to the great interest of these memorials, and expressing the desire that they may (Mr. Sumner assenting) be placed in the capitol.

A letter from Mr. Sumner to Mr. Sparks also accompanies this Message, describing the church at Brington, and some of the associations which cluster around the resting-place of the ancestors of our Washington.  JOHN A. ANDREW.

MR. SPARKS TO THE GOVERNOR.

CAMBRIDGE, 22d February, 1861.

*Dear Sir:* — I enclose a copy of a highly interesting letter from Mr. Charles Sumner, describing the church at Brington, near Althorp, in Northamtonshire. In this church were deposited the remains of Lawrence Washington, who was the father of John and Lawrence Washington, the emigrants to America, and who was therefore the last English ancestor of George Washington. A copy of the inscription on the stone which covers the grave of Lawrence

APPENDIX. 89

Washington, and also of another inscription over the grave of his brother, Robert Washington, who was buried in the same church, are given with exactness in Mr. Sumner's letter. As far as I am aware, these inscriptions are now for the first time made known in this country.

Earl Spencer has sent to Mr. Sumner two stones, being from the same quarry, and having the same form and dimensions, as the originals, and containing a *fac-simile* of the inscriptions. It has been suggested that these stones ought to be placed in the State House, where they may be accessible to the public, and my opinion on the subject has been asked. As they are unquestionably genuine memorials of the Washington family, and possess on this account a singular historical interest, I cannot imagine that a more appropriate disposition of them could be made. I understand that Mr. Sumner would cheerfully assent to such an arrangement, and I cannot doubt that your Excellency will be well inclined to take such measures as may effectually aid in attaining so desirable an object.

I am, Sir, very respectfully yours,

JARED SPARKS.

His Excellency JOHN A. ANDREW,
    *Governor of Massachusetts.*

## MR. SUMNER TO MR. SPARKS.

BOSTON, 22d November, 1860.

*My Dear Sir:*— Since our last conversation Earl Spencer has kindly sent to me precise copies of the two "Memorial Stones" of the English family of George Washington, which I have already described to you as harmonizing exactly with the pedigree which has the sanction of your authority. These are of the same stone, and of the same size, with the originals, and have the original inscriptions,— being in all respects *fac-similes*. They will, therefore, give you an exact idea of those most interesting memorials in the parish-church of Brington, near Althorp, in Northamptonshire.

The largest is of Lawrence Washington, the father of John Washington, who emigrated to America. It is a slab of bluish-gray sandstone, and measures five feet and nine inches long and two feet and six inches broad. Here is the inscription:

HERE·LIETH·THE·BODI·OF·LAVRENCE
WASHINGTON · SONNE · & · HEIRE · OF
ROBERT·WASHINGTON · OF · SOVLGRAE
IN · THE · COVNTIE · OF · NORTHAMPTON
ESQVIER · WHO · MARIED · MARGARET
THE · ELDEST·DAVGHTER·OF·WILLIAM
BVTLER · OF · TEES · IN · THE · COVNTIE
OF · SVSSEXE · ESQVIER ·WHO·HAD·ISSV
BY· HER · 8 · SONNS · & · 9 · DAVGHTERS
WHICH · LAVRENCE ·DECESSED· THE ·13
OF·DECEMBER·A : DÑI : 1616

THOV·THAT·BY·CHANCE·OR·CHOYCE
OF·THIS·HAST·SIGHT
KNOW·LIFE·TO·DEATH·RESIGNES
AS·DAYE·TO·NIGHT
BVT·AS·THE·SVNNS·RETORNE
REVIVES·THE·DAYE
SO·CHRIST·SHALL·VS
THOVGH·TVRNDE·TO·DVST·&·CLAY

Above the inscription carved in the stone, are the arms of the Washingtons, with the arms of the Butlers *impaled*, the latter being, in the language of Heraldry, *azure, a chevron between three covered cups or.*

[Copy of the following Inscrption on page 93.]

The other stone is placed over Robert Washington and Elizabeth his wife. Robert was the uncle of the emigrant. This is a slab of the same sandstone, and measures three feet and six inches long and two feet and six inches broad. The inscription is on a small brass plate set into the stone, and is as follows:

HERE LIES INTERRED Y$^E$ BODIES OF ELIZAB: WASHINGTON WIDDOWE, WHO CHANGED THIS LIFE FOR IMORTALLITIE Y$^E$ 19$^{TH}$ OF MARCH 1622· AS ALSO Y$^E$ BODY OF ROBERT WASHINGTON GENT: HER LATE HVSBAND SECOND SONNE OF ROBERT WASHINGTON OF SOLGRAVE IN Y$^E$ COVNTY OF NORTH: ESQ$^R$: WHO DEPTED THIS LIFE Y$^E$ 10$^{TH}$ OF MARCH 1622· AFTER THEY LIVED LOVINGLY TOGETHER MANY YEARES IN THIS PARRISH

On a separate brass, beneath the inscription, are the arms of the Washingtons without any addition but a crescent, *the mark of cadency* that denotes the *second* son. These as you are well aware, have the combination of stars and stripes, and are sometimes supposed to have suggested our national flag. In heraldic language, they are *argent, two bars gules, in chief three mullets* (or *stars*) *of the second.*

In the interesting chapter on the "Origin and Genealogy of the Washington Family," which you give in the Appendix to your "Life of Washington," it appears that Lawrence, the father of the emigrant, died 13th December, and was buried at Brington 15th December, 1616. But the genealogical tables, which you followed, gave no indication of the locality of this church. Had it appeared that it was the parish-church of the Spencer family, in Northamptonshire, the locality, which I believe, has not been heretofore known in our country, would have been precisely fixed.

In point of fact, the slab which covers Lawrence Washington is in the chancel of the church, by the side of the monuments of the Spencer Family. These are all in admirable preservation, with full-length effigies, busts, or other sculptural work, and exhibit an interesting and connected series of sepulchral memorials, from the reign of Henry the Eighth to the present time. Among them is a monument by the early English sculptor, Nicholas Stone; another by Nollekens from a design by Cipriani; and another by Flaxman, with exquisitely beautiful personifications of Faith and Charity. Beneath repose the successive representatives of this illustrious family, which has added to its aristocratic claims by services to the State, and also by the unique and world-famous library collected by one of its members. In this companionship will be found the last English ancestor of our Washington.

The other slab, covering Robert, the uncle of the

emigrant is in one of the aisles, where it is scraped by the feet of all who pass.

The parish of Brington (in modern pronunciation *Brighton*) is between seven and eight miles from the town of Northampton, not far from the centre of England. It is written in Domesday Book "Brinintone" and also "Brintone." It contains about 2,210 acres, of which about 1,490 belong to Earl Spencer, about 326 acres to the rector in right of his church, and about 130 acres to other persons. The soil is in general a dark-colored loam, with a small tract of clay towards the north. Nearly four-fifths of the whole is pasture and feeding land.

In the village still stands the house said to have been occupied by the Washingtons when the emigrant brother left them. You will see a vignette of it on the title page of the recent English work, entitled *The Washingtons*. Over the door are carved the words, THE LORD GEVETH, THE LORD TAKETH AWAY, BLESSED BE THE NAME OF THE LORD; while the Parish Register gives a pathetic commentary by showing, that, in the very year when this house was built, a child had been born and another had died in this family.

The church, originally dedicated to the Virgin,

stands at the north-east angle of the village, and consists of an embattled tower with five bells, a nave, north and south aisles, a chancel, a chapel, and a modern porch. The tower is flanked by buttresses of two stages. The present fabric goes back in its origin to the beginning of the fourteenth century, nearly two hundred years before the discovery of America. The chancel and chapel, where repose the Spencers and Lawrence Washington, were rebuilt by Sir John Spencer, the purchaser of the estate, at the beginning of the sixteenth century. They afford one of the latest specimens of the Tudor style of architecture. The church is beautifully "situated on the summit of the highest ground of Brington," and is surrounded by a stone wall, lined with trees. Dibdin says that a more complete picture of a country churchyard is rarely seen. A well-trimmed walk encircles the whole of the interior, while the fine Gothic windows at the end of the chancel fill the scene with picturesque beauty.

The Register of the Parish, which is still preserved, commences in 1560. From this it appears that William Proctor was the rector from 1601 to 1627, covering the period of the last of the Washingtons there. The following further entries occur, relating to this family:

1616. "Mr. Lawrance Washington was buried the XVth day of December."
1620. "Mr. Philip Curtis and M$^{is}$ Amy Washington were married August 8."
1622. "Mr. Robert Washington was buried March y$^e$ 11th."
———. "M$^{rs}$. Elisabeth Washington widow was buried March y$^e$ 20th."

Of one of the ministers in this church we have an interesting glimpse in Evelyn's Memoirs (Vol. I., p. 652), where the following entry will be found under date of August 18th, 1688: "Dr. Jeffryes [a misnomer for *Jessop*], the minister of Althorp, who was my Lord's chaplain when Ambassador in France, *preached the shortest discourse I ever heard;* but what was defective in the amplitude of his sermon, he had supplied in the largeness and convenience of the parsonage house."

At a short distance — less than a mile — is Althorp, the seat of the Spencers, surrounded by a park of five hundred acres, of which one of the gates opens near the church. There are oak trees, bordering on the church-yard, which were growing at the time of the purchase of the estate, in the reign of

Henry the Seventh. Evelyn was often here a delighted visitor. On one occasion he speaks of "the house, or rather palace, at Althorp." (Vol. I., p. 652.) In another place he describes it as "placed in a pretty open bottom, very finely watered, and flanked with stately woods and groves in a park." (Vol. I., p. 478.) Let me add, that there is an engraving of Althorp at this time, by the younger Luke Vorsterman, a Dutch artist.

There is one feature of the park which excited the admiration of Evelyn, and at a later day of Mrs. Jameson, who gives to it some beautiful pages in her "Visits and Sketches at home and abroad." It is the record of the times when different plantations of trees were begun. While recommending this practice in his "Sylva," Evelyn remarks, "The only instance I know of the like in our country is in the park of Althorp." There are six of these commemorative stones. The first records a wood planted by Sir John Spencer, in 1567 and 1568; the second, a wood planted by Sir John Spencer, son of the former, in 1589; the third, a wood planted by Robert Lord Spencer, in 1602 and 1603; the fourth, a wood planted by Sir William Spencer, Knight of the Bath, afterwards Lord Spencer, in 1624. This stone is ornamented with the arms of the Spencers, and on the back is inscribed, VP AND BEE DOING AND GOD WILL PROSPER. It was in this scenery, and amidst these associations, that the Washingtons lived. When the emigrant left in 1657, these woods must have been well-grown. It was not long afterwards that they arrested the attention of Evelyn.

The Household Books at Althorp show, that for many years the Washingtons were frequent guests there. The hospitality of this seat has been renowned. The Queen of James the First and Prince Henry, on their way to London in 1603, were welcomed there in an entertainment, memorable for a Masque from the vigorous muse of Ben Jonson. (Ben Jonson's Works, Vol. VI., p. 475.) Charles the First was at Althorp in 1647, when he received the first intelligence of the approach of those pursuers from whom he never escaped until his life had been laid down upon the scaffold. In 1695, King William was there for a week, and, according to Evelyn, was "mightily entertained." (Vol. II., p. 30.) At least one of the members of this family was famous for hospitality of a different character. Evelyn records that he used to dine with the Countess of Sunderland, — the title then borne by the Spencers, —

"when she invited *fire-eaters*, stone-eaters, and opera-singers, after the fashion of the day." (Vol. I., pp. 458, 483, 579.)

The family was early and constantly associated with literature; Spencer, the poet, belonged to it, and to one of its members he has dedicated his "Tears of the Muses." It was for the same Alice Spencer that Milton is said to have written his "Arcades," and Sir John Harrington has celebrated her memory by an epigram. The Sacharissa of Waller was the Lady Dorothy Sidney, wife of the first Earl of Sunderland, the third Lord Spencer, who perished fighting for King Charles the First at Newbury. I do not dwell on other associations of a later day, as my object is simply to allude to those which existed in the time of the Washingtons.

"The Nobility of the Spencers has been illustrated and enriched by the trophies of Marlborough; but I exhort them to consider the Fairy Queen as the most precious jewel of their coronet." Thus wrote Gibbon in his Memoirs, and all must feel the beauty of the passage. Perhaps it is not too much to say that this nobility may claim another illustration from its ties of friendship and neighborhood with the family of Washington. I cannot doubt that hereafter the parish-church of Brington will be often visited by our countrymen, who will look with reverence upon a spot so closely associated with American history.

I trust that this little sketch, suggested by what I saw at Althorp during a brief visit last autumn, will not seem irrelevant. Besides my own personal impressions and the volumes quoted, I have relied upon Dibdin's "Ædes Althorpianæ," so interesting to all bibliographical students, and especially upon Baker's "History of Northamptonshire," — one of those magnificent local works which illustrate English history — to which you refer in your Appendix.

Of course, the Memorial Stones, which I have received from Lord Spencer, are of much historic value; and I think that I shall best carry out the generous idea of the giver by taking care that they are permanently placed where they can be seen by the public; perhaps in the State House near Chantrey's beautiful statue of Washington,— if this should be agreeable to the Commonwealth.

Pray pardon this long letter, and believe me, my dear Sir, with much regard,

    Ever sincerely yours,
        CHARLES SUMNER.

JARED SPARKS, Esq.

## COMMONWEALTH OF MASSACHUSETTS.

HOUSE OF REPRESENTATIVES, March 23, 1861.

The Committee on the State House, to whom was referred the Message of His Excellency the Governor, presenting to the General Court, as a gift from the Hon. Charles Sumner, certain memorials of Washington, of great historic interest, report that they consider it a matter of special congratulation that the interesting facts concerning the Father of his Country, contained in the papers accompanying the Message, should have been first made known to us by a citizen of Massachusetts; and, deeming it important that these valuable memorials should be permanently preserved in the capitol of the State, they report the accompanying resolves.

Per order,<br>R. WARD.

RESOLVES in relation to certain Memorials of the Ancestors of Washington.

*Resolved*, That the thanks of the General Court be and hereby are presented to the Hon. Charles

Sumner for his interesting and patriotic gift to the Commonwealth, of two Memorial Tablets in imitation of the originals which mark the final resting-place of the last English ancestors of GEORGE WASHINGTON.

*Resolved*, That the Commissioners on the State House cause the same to be prepared and placed, with appropriate inscriptions, in some convenient place in the Doric Hall of the State House, near the Statue of Washington. —*Approved, April* 6, 1861.

---

OFFICE OF THE COMMISSIONERS ON THE STATE HOUSE,
BOSTON, January 1, 1862.

The undersigned, commissioners on the State House, hereby certify, that, in compliance with the Resolve of the Legislature of Massachusetts, passed April 6, 1861, they have caused the above-named Memorial Tablets of the Washington Family to be permanently placed upon the marble floor of the area in which the Statue of Washington stands, within the railing in front of said Statue.

JOHN MORISSEY, *Sergeant-at-Arms*.
OLIVER WARNER, *Secretary*.
HENRY K. OLIVER, *Treasurer*.

A white marble tablet, placed by the Commissioners near the Washington Memorials, bears the following inscription:

THESE FAC-SIMILES OF THE MEMORIAL STONES OF THE WASHINGTON FAMILY IN THE PARISH CHURCH OF BRINGTON, THE BURIAL-PLACE OF THE SPENCERS NEAR ALTHORP, NORTHAMPTONSHIRE, ENGLAND, WERE PRESENTED BY THE RIGHT HONORABLE EARL SPENCER TO CHARLES SUMNER OF MASSACHUSETTS, AND BY HIM OFFERED TO THE COMMONWEALTH 22 FEBRUARY, 1861.

LAWRENCE WAS FATHER, AND ROBERT UNCLE, OF THE ENGLISH EMIGRANT TO VIRGINIA, WHO WAS GREAT-GRANDFATHER OF GEORGE WASHINGTON.

## XX.

### VERSES BY BISHOP BERKELEY,

"ON THE

Prospect of planting ARTS and LEARNING in *America.*"

"First Printed A. D. MDCCXXXV."

THE Muse, disgusted at an Age and Clime,
    Barren of every glorious Theme,
In distant Lands now waits a better Time,
    Producing Subjects worthy Fame:

In happy Climes, where from the genial Sun
    And virgin Earth such Scenes ensue,
The Force of Art by Nature seems outdone,
    And fancied Beauties by the true:

In happy Climes the Seat of Innocence,
    Where Nature guides and Virtue rules,
Where Men shall not impose for Truth and Sense,
    The Pedantry of Courts and Schools:

There shall be sung another golden Age,
    The rise of Empire and of Arts,
The Good and Great inspiring epic Rage,
    The wisest Heads and noblest Hearts.

Not such as *Europe* breeds in her decay;
    Such as she bred when fresh and young,
When heav'nly Flame did animate her clay,
    By future Poets shall be sung.

Westward the Course of Empire takes its Way;
    The four first Acts already past,
A fifth shall close the Drama with the Day;
    Time's noblest Offspring is the last.

# A POETICAL EPISTLE

TO

# GEORGE WASHINGTON, Esq.,

*COMMANDER-IN-CHIEF OF THE ARMIES OF THE
UNITED STATES OF AMERICA.*

BY

REV. CHARLES HENRY WHARTON, D. D.

---

FROM THE ORIGINAL MANUSCRIPT BELONGING TO

DAVID PULSIFER, A. M.,

MEMBER OF THE NEW ENGLAND HISTORIC-GENEALOGICAL SOCIETY, FELLOW OF THE AMERICAN STATISTICAL ASSOCIATION, CORRESPONDING MEMBER OF THE ESSEX INSTITUTE, AND OF THE RHODE ISLAND, NEW YORK, CONNECTICUT, AND WISCONSIN HISTORICAL SOCIETIES.

WITH AN APPENDIX.

BOSTON:
PRINTED FOR DAVID PULSIFER.
FOR SALE BY A. WILLIAMS & CO.,
283 WASHINGTON STREET.
1881.

www.ingramcontent.com/pod-product-compliance
Lightning Source LLC
Chambersburg PA
CBHW020143170426
43199CB00010B/871